D0933790

BYRON NELSON

THE LITTLE BLACK BOOK

Byron Nelson

THE LITTLE BLACK BOOK

The personal diary of golf legend Byron Nelson

1935-1947

including the year of his record eleven straight

tournament victories.

with tips, stories, and reflections from

Sam Snead, Arnold Palmer, Kathy Whitworth,

Henry Picard, Tom Watson, Ken Venturi,

Mickey Wright, Don January, Jug McSpaden,

and other golf greats

FOREWORD BY HARVEY PENICK

THE SUMMIT PUBLISHING GROUP • ARLINGTON, TEXAS

THE SUMMIT PUBLISHING GROUP

One Arlington Center
1112 East Copeland Road, Fifth Floor
Arlington, Texas 76011

95   96   97   98   5   4   3   2   I

Library of Congress Cataloging-in-Publication Data

Nelson, Byron, 1912-
    Byron Nelson : the little black book : the personal diary of
golf legend Byron Nelson ; 1935-1947, including the year of
his record eleven straight tournament victories / foreword by
Harvey Penick ; with special commentary from Sam Snead...
[et al.].
        p. cm.
    ISBN: I-56530-180-3 (alk. paper)
    I. Nelson, Byron, 1912-   —Diaries. 2. Golfers—United
States—Diaries.   I. Title.
GV964.N45A3   1995
796.352'092 B—dc20   95-15760
                                                  CIP

Book design by David Sims

Photography: AP/Wide World Photos

*T*o my many golfing friends
all over the country

FOREWORD

I am happy to commend to you Byron Nelson and his book. For sixty years, I've liked and admired him for a number of reasons.

Back in the thirties, a lot of us who tried to teach people to play golf became fascinated with Byron's golf swing. Steel shafts had just replaced hickory, and Byron seemed to have found the way to get the most out of the new clubs. I'd study him in play or practice; his swing seemed perfect, his balance was perfect, even his divots (which looked like little dollar bills) were perfect in a certain way.

And like everybody else, I was amazed at what Byron did in his great year of 1945. Eleven straight wins and eighteen tournament victories for the year. It's still hard for me to believe that anyone could play so well for such a long period of time. It's a wonderful thing when success finds a man as nice as Byron Nelson.

But as much as I was impressed by his swing and his great record as a tournament player, I've treasured our friendship much more. I think the big thing we have in common is that we love people more than golf.

HARVEY PENICK
Austin, Texas

Acknowledgments

Putting together any book is a monumental task, and I would like to thank the following people for their significant contributions to the book:

To my wife, Peggy, who as usual has been a tireless guiding light in helping me get this project together in what so far has been a whirlwind 1995;

To my golfing friends Sam Snead, Arnold Palmer, Henry Picard, Tom Watson, Jackie Burke, Jr., Ken Venturi, Jug McSpaden, Kathy Whitworth, Harvey Penick, Dave Marr, Mickey Wright, Don January, and Marilynn Smith for taking the time to offer their kind and insightful remarks to this book;

To my good friend Bill Inglish, retired *Daily Oklahoman* sportswriter and for thirty-two years the chief statistician for the Masters. Bill's tireless work with numbers has always fascinated me;

To my accountant Jon Bradley, whose encouragement and guidance made this book possible;

To writer Curt Sampson, who in two weeks crunched thirteen interviews with my golfing friends while compiling the excellent commentary in this book;

To editor Mike Towle of The Summit Publishing Group for his diligence and care in shepherding this book through the publishing process;

And to all of my many friends and acquaintances who have been with me through the years. Thank you for your friendship.

INTRODUCTION

I really don't know why I started keeping my little black notebook in 1935, except that it must have had something to do with my love for figures—numbers and statistics. I still like playing with numbers. I don't play the stock market, but I like to follow it just to see all the figures.

In 1943 and part of 1944, fellow golfer Jug McSpaden and I spent a lot of time together on trains, crisscrossing the country to play in various wartime exhibitions. We were classified 4-F, meaning we couldn't pass the army physical to serve our country in World War II. While sitting on the train with Jug, I would play around with figures to help pass the time. I specifically remember coming up with a figure of $100,000 when calculating how much money we would need to be able to retire comfortably. How times have changed.

That's what *The Little Black Book* is all about—figures. It's not a detailed diary, nor is it a complicated statistical analysis. It is a compilation of basic notes, figures, and facts that I kept during my twelve years as a full-time touring golf professional. The book encompasses the years 1935 through 1946 (with a bit of 1947 included for good measure, because that one page from 1947 remains in the original black notebook). I recorded every round and every tournament in which I played from 1935 through 1946. I've talked to a lot of players since then and know of no one who has done this.

The Little Black Book is a remembrance book, a scrapbook of sorts, featuring photographed copies of the actual pages from my black notebook. When I first set pen to paper sixty years ago, there was no way I could have known how important to me this notebook would be. Likewise, there was no way in 1945 that I could have even imagined my best year in golf would be the object of so much attention fifty years later. But it is.

As it turned out, my strict adherence to record keeping played a major role in the great year of golf I had in 1945. While reviewing my notebook records after the 1944 season, I concluded two things: 1) I wasn't concentrating as well as I could, and 2) my chipping wasn't as good as it needed to be. Reading my written notes, as well as recalling everything "between the lines," told me this. With notebook in hand, I resolved to make 1945 my best year yet. I would focus better on the golf course and be more consistently accurate with my chips around the green. Call this my New Year's resolution  for 1945, because I resolved this right around Christmastime. The rest, as they say, is history.

Still, I knew that I was going to miss shots. All golfers do. I couldn't eliminate that because I'm human. But the thing I could eliminate was *throwing away* shots. In looking back over my 1944 season, I counted about ten or twelve times where I had remembered chipping badly. So I worked on my chipping before we started the tour in 1945 and made up my mind that I wasn't going to play a careless shot.

In 1945 I ended up lowering my per-round stroke average from 69.67 to 68.33. That equals one-and-one-third strokes per round. That works out to five strokes over the course of a tournament, and that's a lot.

I also had a very good year in 1944, winning eight tournaments. At the time, I guess I would have been justified in thinking that I had had a good year, and just let it go at that. But my goal was not only to be the leading money winner, but also to win every important tournament in the United States at least once, lower my stroke average, and be in the money more than anyone else. I don't mean to sound arrogant here. I'm just being honest in expressing my heartfelt goals of fifty years ago, and every good golfer has lofty goals.

The only way you can improve your game is by taking the bad parts of your game and changing them. It's just as if you're sinning in some way. You can't keep doing it; you just have to quit. It's the same thing in golf; quit doing the bad things. That is what I did.

Because of 1945, nineteen ninety-five has been more exciting than I ever thought it could be for a man who is, like me, in his eighties. I have had dozens of interviews and appearances, and have had to do something I don't like doing very often—saying no. But golfing buffs everywhere still want to talk to me about 1945, and I'm only too happy to oblige. That is why I am making *The Little Black Book* available to everyone now, so you can see a lot of my personal golf history for yourself.

Of course, showing you the actual pages from my little black notebook is only part of the story. Throughout the book, I have added some anecdotes and commentary relative not only to the actual tournaments and events mentioned, but also to the lessons of golf that have been timeless for me. I hope they will work for you as well.

I am also grateful to my many friends in golf who have volunteered their time to add their own comments to this work. I figured having other golfing greats sharing their own stories and golf analysis in this book would give readers a more in-depth and objective look at the game and at Byron Nelson. I trust you will agree.

BYRON NELSON
Roanoke, Texas

1935

I didn't realize it at the time, but when my father taught me to play golf many years ago, a lot of what he taught was Byron Nelson. A deliberate backswing, a **complete** weight shift, and a hard hit; that was Byron's way and, eventually, my way. Not that our swings looked identical. But those were the fundamentals that worked for both of us.

Nothing compares to Byron's eleven-tournament winning streak. I won three in a row in 1960 and in 1962; Snead, Hogan, Tom Watson, Johnny Miller, and a few others have also won three straight. Jack Burke, Jr. won four in a row. Then there's Byron's eleven in a row...A lot of things, like the press and the pressure, will prevent anyone from breaking that *record. But one of the biggest reasons that record is safe is the rarity of players with his skill.*

One other thing I was taught by my father was that golf is a game for gentlemen. And I can't think of a nicer gentleman in our sport than Byron Nelson. I'm only sorry we were from different generations...It would have been fun to compete against him.

—ARNOLD PALMER

Putting

As I noted in regard to the 1935 Metropolitan Open, I putted very poorly. I had fifteen three-putt greens and one four-putt hole. The grasses from course to course varied greatly in those days, but that wasn't the problem when it came to my putting. My problem was me. It had to be.

You are going to three-putt some holes, but if you are three-putting a lot, then you need to do some work in two areas: 1) work on your short

My Tournament record 1935

Riverside   Pro- Amateur

Score   Place   money
  64   2nd-Tie   125.00

Los Angeles Open
Played bad all thru -
74-75-80-74 - 303

San Frisco match play
146 qualified 6 th
Beat Lawson Little   5-4
Beat Vic Ghezzie   3-2
Lost to Mac Spalding 6-4
won   154.00

Sacramento Open
75-72-80-80 - 307
Played all shots bad.

putts, and 2) work on your lag putts—which is related to the speed in which you are hitting the ball. I don't care what kind of break you have on the green or how well you read it; if you have the wrong speed on your putt, you're not going to make it. You have to have your ball slowing down as it approaches the hole on a breaking putt.

McSpaden was a wonderful putter. Then he got the yips and putted badly. Once he got over the yips—and not all golfers do, even the good ones—he played great. The idea is not to get defensive about your putting to the point where you're playing to avoid three-putts when you should be trying to hole all your makeable putts.

Playing to Win

I played in thirty-one tournaments in 1935 and won $3,246, which averages out to about one hundred dollars a week. That came close to covering my expenses, but not quite. The mistake I

Glen Dale Open
Shot 297. Played irons
very bad thru out.

Aqua Coliente Open
Pulled very bad 3rd round
72-71-76-72- 291
won 6th tie $257.00

Phoenix Open
Played last 9 holes bad
72-73- 71- 74- 290
was 10th and $75.00

Charleston Open
Played well all thru
73-71- 70-70- 284
won 6th and $100.00
had 7 on par 4 no. 4 on
last round.

made early in my career was figuring that to make expenses, I would have to finish in the top ten. I didn't realize it at first, but playing well enough to cover your expenses is setting your sights too low.

When you start figuring you need to finish in the top ten, that's all you'll do when you're playing well. A lot of golf is attitude. If you set your goal to average 73 in a round, that's what you will average—if you work hard enough. If your goal is 70, then you will gear your work toward that. It took me a while to get the idea that if you're going to win tournaments, you have to set winning as your goal, and not accept less.

Keeping Your Swing Consistent

As you can see by my scores at the 1935 Medinah Open and the General Brock tournament the following week, my game still wasn't consistent. I was having one bad round nearly every tournament,

Pinehurst N+S Open
Played very bad last two
rounds. Especially irons.
71-69- 77-76- 293
won 12th and $60.00

Atlanta. Open
Terrible rain on 2nd round
78-75- 69- 215
won 3rd and $250.00

Augusta Nat'l. Open
Played last 3 holes bad
74-72-71- 74 - 291
won 8th-tie-and $137.50

Metropolitan Open
Putted very bad. 15-3-1-4
76-76-77-77- 306

and that continued through most of the year. Somewhere and somehow, I was losing my focus during some rounds. I suppose that was in part because of the fact that I was still working on the fundamentals of my game, and wasn't yet comfortable with my swing. I might have been thinking more about the technical aspects of swing instead of the strategical aspects on which all winners focus.

At this point, I was still working on taking the club straight back and straight through. Sometimes I would move ahead of the ball or ahead of the shot, and would end up pushing the ball out toward the right. It's not that I was trying to steer the ball, I just wasn't being consistent with my swing and follow-through.

KEEPING YOUR HEAD

Note under the entry for the 1935 National Open at Oakmont, where I wrote, "Played well,

Medinah Open – 72
78 – 73 – 77 – 73 – 301
tied for 12th. won $62.50
General Brock Open = 70
72 – 71 – 72 – 77 – 292
won 2nd Place + $600.00

St. Paul Open. – 72
July 19-20-21
72 – 76 – 73 – 76 – 297

Was it over Par 1st. 6 holes
on the 1st rounds.

New Jersey Pro. amt.
One day
tied First
$10.40

but no head work. Failed to qualify by one stroke."

You're probably wondering what I meant by "head work." I'm not referring to the part of the golf club that strikes the ball. Rather, I'm talking about head work of the cerebral variety. I wasn't thinking right that week; I wasn't concentrating.

I remember one hole—the fifteenth—where I put the ball way out to the right in some rough that hadn't even been mowed. It was as high as a desk. The hole doglegged to the left. I had aimed my tee shot a little to the right because I was hooking the ball then, but I hit it too hard and pushed it right. I made an eight on that hole and ended up playing it badly the next day, too.

The biggest problem I had in those days was my driving. I hit the ball far enough, but I was inconsistent. If you have an idea that you are going to consistently hook the ball too much, you get to know how to guard against it. Or if you fade all the time, you know how to compensate. Where you get into trouble is when you get to the

N. Jersey State Open
        8 - 8-9-10- 35
75-71- 70- 72 - 288
won by 3 strokes
won $400.00
Also won   40.00 Bonus.

True Temper Open
    8 -   16-17-18

75 - 76 - 75 - 79 - 305
No money

Hershey Open
    8 - 22-23- 24 - 25
71 - 74 -73 - 78 - 296
Tied for 6th. won $143.75

tee not knowing if it's going to go left or right. That's when you're in trouble and that was too often my problem.

Ben Hogan was a great player. In the early stages of his career, he would hook his shots, even with a nine-iron. He would hit toward the right of the green and the shot would end up straight to the flagstick almost every time. I remember one year he won the San Francisco Match Play tournament, where there were a lot of trees along the right side of the holes. Ben couldn't use his driver and play his hook with those trees, so he used a four-wood with which he would hit out over the trees and draw the ball back into the fairway.

GETTING YOUR (CLUB) HEAD IN THE GAME

What was happening to me with my drivers made me learn to think better about my game. I ended up buying four different drivers in 1935, but none

Philadelphia - P. G. A. -
75 - 75 - 73 - 223
One stroke out of money -
Played badly

Nat'l Open at Oakmont. 72
75 - 81 - 82 - 77 - 315
Played well but no
head work. Failed to qualify
by one stroke.

Swackly Open 72
74 - 78 - 152
Played irons badly

Western Open 72
75 - 72 - 74 - 75 - 296
Won 3rd and $200.00
Played well except No 16
had 8 - 4 - 6 - 6. 4 balls in
the water.

- 13 -

of them looked quite right to me. I had done a little club work for Ted Longworth back at Glen Garden Country Club (in Fort Worth) when I was a caddie and junior member there. Back then, everybody worked on his own clubs. I picked out the driver I liked best of the four and went to work.

I smoothed off the face of the club a little on the heel and a little on the toe. All clubs are made that way now, but they were all straight across the face then, making you hook the ball if you hit it a little off the toe and slice if you hit it off the heel. Taking a little bit off the heel and toe eliminated some of that. I went to the practice tee and it looked great to me. I hit the ball well with it that way and used only three drivers over the rest of my career.

Glen Falls, Open
Sept. 8 - 9 - 10 -
74 - 72 - 71 - 73 - 290
tied for 11th
won $56.00
Putted Terrible
Baltimore, Md.
Calvert Open

Sept 13 - 14 - 15
76 - 73 - 75 - 71 - 295
won $25.00 Sixth
Putted Terrible

PGC Qualifying
80 - 76 -
failed

Sport 18 - 19 -

Jersey P.G.A. -
71 - 74 - 71 - 75 = 291
tied and lost on 2nd
play off. 75 - 73 -
won $ 100.00

Oct. 3 - 4 - 5 - 6
Indianapolis open
80 - 75 Failed to
qualify. Putted terrible.
14 three putts on 36 holes.

Oct. 10 - 11 - 12 - 13
Louisville Open
71 - 74 - 72 - 72 - $ 362.50
Orlando Fla. Dec. 5 - 6 - 7 -
72 - 75 - 73 - 77 - 297
Sarasota, Fla. Dec. 9 - 10 - 11 -
73 - 69 - 68 - 77 - 287

8,746.75
2,746.75

Miami Fla.^{Dec.} - 14 - 19

70 - 72 - 77 - 75 - 294

won 37.⁵⁰

Pasadena Open

Dec. - 26 - 30 - 35

71 - 75 - 73 - 71 - 290

won $50.⁰⁰

Played in 31 tournaments

Winning $3,246.40

Paid by Spalding 1,500.00

" " Geo. 400.00
_____

$5,146.40

~~Cash on Hand 1-1-36~~

Net profit for 1935 = 1,200.⁰⁰

12 won no money

19 " $3,246.40

- 17 -

1935

What I win in Tournaments

Western Open	$ 200.00
Medinah	62.50
General Brock	600.00
Jersey State	450.00
Hershey	143.75
~~Dixie~~	6.00
Calvert	25.00
Jersey PGA	100.00
Louisville	362.50
Miami	37.50
Pasadena	$ 50.00
Start 1935	$ 2,087.75
Riverside	128.00
Frisco	154.00
Caliente	257.50
Phoenix	75.00
Charleston	100.00
Pinehurst	60.00
Atlanta	250.00
Augusta	127.50
Total	$ 3,246.40

my average score for
the year 72 $\frac{107}{115}$

1936

Byron would "work" every ball he hit. It gave him delight to control the ball; all the early players took delight in executing shots the way they needed to. They had to, because there wasn't enough money in the game to have the satisfaction of getting rich.

Nelson was a master with the hands. Hands first, then the body follows; great swings come from great hands. He wasn't afraid to move his head a little bit, but the club and Byron returned

My Tournament Record
for the year 1936 - ad.
Riverside Calif.
Jan.   3 - 4 - 5 - 1936
72 - 69 - 71 - 74 - 286
Tied 3rd. won $300.00

Los Angeles Open
Jan.   10 - 11 - 12 - 1936
68 - 72 - 72 - 75 - 287
won 7th and $200.00

Sacramento, Open!
Jan.   17 - 18 - 19 - 1936
75 - 69 - 71 - 72 - 287
won 3rd + $350.00

San Francisco Open
74 - 73 - 147
Was 16th won $52.50

Santa Catalina
Jan. 30 - 31 - 1st Feb.
65 - 65 - 64 - 65 - 259
Was 6th and won 208.34

- 21 -

to the ball at the same time. The distance he stood from the ball was very important to him...His feel, timing, and balance were so good.

Our paths didn't cross in tournaments too much, but he knew my dad real well. Byron was very friendly. I admired him a lot.

As for winning a lot of tournaments in a row [Burke won four consecutively in 1952, the second longest streak in PGA Tour history], you don't think it will ever happen. I remember reminding myself that my clubs didn't know I'd won the week before. During a streak, you'd find lots of reasons you'd want to get away from it: you're tired, it's cold or freezing, or it's raining. You're like a horse that wants to go back to the barn. So you have to have a meeting with yourself. I'm sure Byron did that; he didn't consider last week, he just kept firing. He could hit **every** fairway and **every** green. **Rarely** did he make a mistake.

The only people I can compare to Nelson are [Jack] Nicklaus, who just circled the track with

Thomasville Ga.
Feb. 14-15-16-
75 - 75 -   150
Sick in bed last day

St. Petersburg Fla.
Feb 20-21- 22
71 - 79 - 73 - 69 - 292
won 12th $ 55.00

Hollywood, Fla.
Mar. 3-4- 5
71 - 73 - 72 - 71 - 287
Was 22 nd.
Mar. 12-13-14-15-16-
St. Augustine Pro-Amateur.
Qualified with - 143
won 1st match from Revolta 3-2
lost 2nd to Shazzi   2-1
won $50.00

his twenty majors, Hogan, [Sam] Snead, and
Roberto [DeVicenzo]. You know you have to be
extremely selfish to win like those guys did, but
Byron was anointed with a pleasing personality.
—JACK BURKE, JR.

TOO MUCH PRACTICE ISN'T THE ANSWER

After 1936, I practiced very little, a fact which nobody really understood back then. I practiced some, but certainly not like some of the guys who play today. You see these young guys out there today hitting two hundred, three hundred, four hundred or more balls a day on the practice tee. Now, I really don't understand that.

I found that after I became a pretty good player, I was happy with the way I was swinging. I wouldn't say I was happy with the way I was scoring, but I was swinging the club well and striking the ball like I wanted to. I was hitting the ball

Charleston - Mar - 18 - 21 -
75 - 71 - 77 - 73 - 296
tied for 11 th. won $75.00

Pinehurst 24 - 25 - 26 - 27
79 - 75 - 76 - 76 - 306
april.
Augusta National - 3 - 4-5 -
76 - 71   - 77 - 74 - 298
tied 12th won $50.00

Met. Open - 5 - 21 - 22 - 36
71 - 69 - 72 - 71 - 283
won by two strokes
Prize of $750.00

solidly and hitting it straight, so I didn't see the wisdom of spending a lot of time on the tee tinkering with my swing.

That's not to say in looking back that *had* I practiced more in those days I would have learned earlier on to concentrate better. But I wasn't going to force myself to do something just because other golfers were practicing more than me. Ben Hogan once made mention of my lack of practice during a 1940 radio interview, which I'll get into in more detail later in the book.

Control Your Anger

By the time the summer of 1936 rolled around, I was starting to play a lot better. I headed out to the Pacific Northwest tour, where I played in four tournaments and won a total of twenty-six hundred dollars. That gave me a lot of confidence, although I learned something during that stretch of play that I have never forgotten.

Natl. Open. 6- 4-5-6-36
79- 74- 153
Failed to Qualify

Shawnee Open - 6- 7-8-9-
72-71- 73- 74- 290
tied for 4th.
won $226.66

General Brock Open
6-11-12- 13 - 36

74-72 - 76- 74- 296
Tenth won $140.00

Ill. State Open
75 - 69 - 144
7th. won 21.66

In the first tournament of that Pacific Northwest swing (I think it was in Vancouver), I was playing quite well tee to green—especially with my irons. But I wasn't putting well. In the final round, I had good birdie putts on each of the first five holes, only to miss them all. Frustrated, I finally flung my putter up into one of those evergreen trees. No spectators were there to see it, but that didn't matter. I was ashamed of myself.

I was taught by my parents not to let anger get the better of me. The Bible says you can get mad, but that you should never let the sun go down on your anger. Although I was able to release my anger that one time by throwing my club, I suggest you find a better way.

One way to avoid losing your temper is to understand your human physiology. The trick is to not put yourself in a position to get angry, regardless of how many bad shots or bad holes you have. The main thing you want to watch is how fast you are moving while playing. If you walk faster than your normal pace, your heart is

6- 19-21- 36

Western Open.

69- 72- 72- 65 - 278

3rd. won. $200-

St. Paul open

7 - 16- 17- 18 - 36

68- 72- 71- 70 - 281

tie 5 & 6, & 7th - $306.33

Vancouver B. C -

7 - 23 - 25 - 36

70 - 70- 72- 66 - 278

tied part 5th money $975.

Victoria B. C.

7- 27- 29- 36

64- 68 - 69- 71 - 272

2nd won $450.

going to beat faster, your swing is going to get too quick, and your timing isn't going to be any good. A quickened heartbeat can make you prone to anger. Think about it. I tell a lot of people that when it comes to dealing with pressure, learn to breathe slowly and deeply. Don't let your breath get any faster. Force yourself to walk more slowly and to take deeper, slower breaths. It will help your game and help you control your temper.

ADRENALINE RUSH

If you are a good competitor—and everybody likes to win—you know what it's like to get the adrenaline going. Then you get steamed up. Your heart beats faster. Next thing you know, you're doing everything too fast.

In my playing days, you had the gallery walking with you. You hit a shot and then they'd start running. Next thing you know, you're keeping pace with the gallery and are out of breath by the

7-31 - 8-1-2-36
Seattle, Washington
73-74 - 74 - 73 - 293
7th won $270.

Portland, Oregon
8 - 8-9- 10 - 36
71 - 68 - 71 - 72 - 282
7th won $250.00

Glen Falls
8 - 28-29-30-36
66 - 73 - 75 - 70 - 284
won 3rd $400.

Hershey, Penna.
9 - 3-4-5-6- 36
73-74-73 -73-293
Tied 9th. Won $180.00

time you get to your ball to hit your next shot. I've even had someone in the gallery step on me, tripping me and knocking me to the ground.

One time in the British Open, I was walking along with my driver under my arm. A man rushed by, hit my foot, and caught my club, knocking me to the ground. I ended up going to the chiropractor three straight days just so I could finish the tournament. You don't run into things like that anymore, but players can still wind up walking faster than their normal pace in a pressure situation and that isn't always good.

Watch great players such as Watson, Nicklaus, Fred Couples, and Nick Price. Notice that they, too, get faster when they are charging. You can see it in their walk. One time my first wife, Louise, and I were watching Nicklaus and Watson battling it out in the Masters Tournament on TV. Nicklaus would birdie, then Watson would. Back and forth it went. Louise was saying, "Slow down, Jack, slow down. Don't walk so fast." He was charging.

Sept. 10-11-12 —
Canadian Open
72-71-75-69- 287
tied 10th. won $42.00
N.J. S. Pro amateur.
Lost semi final - 1 up 21
won $55.00
N.J. L. P.S.a.
3 at won $75.00

Nat'l. P.G.a.
Failed to qualify
80-78- 158

Augusta Open
71-71-74-73- 289
tied for 14th
won $6.75

Miami Billt. More
78- 76- 72- 77= 300
no money.

Played in 27
won $5798.75
on average of $214.76 per
tournament.

won money in 24 out
of 27.

Tournament Winnings for 1926

Riverside, Calif.	✓	$ 300.00
Los Angeles, "	✓	200.00
Sacramento "	✓	350.00
San Frisco "	✓	52.50
Catalina "	✓	208.34
Pro Amateur (Lakeside)		30.00
St. Petersburg	✓	55.00
St. Augustine	✓	50.00
Charleston	✓	75.00
Augusta	✓	50.00
Metropolitan Open	✓	750.00
Shawnee Open	✓	226.66
General Brock	?	140.00
I.U. State		21.66
Western	✓	200.00
St. Paul	✓	306.33
Vancouver	✓	975.00
Victoria	✓	450.35
Total		4440.49

- 35 -

Tournament winnings "1936"

Seattle	270.00
Portland	250.00
Glen Falls	400.00
Hershey	180.00
Comedian	42.00
N.Y. P.G.A.	75.00
1 Prw.Am.	55.00
Augusta	86.25

$ 5,798.75
500.00
1000.00
1500.00
$ 7.898.75

1937

hen I made the Ryder Cup team in 1965 [by virtue of winning the 1965 PGA Championship], it was the first time the players voted for the captain. Someone—I don't remember who—said Byron's name, and the vote for him was unanimous. Winnie Palmer, Arnold's wife, came up with the greatest idea: She had a gold replica of the Ryder Cup trophy

made and had all of us (me, Palmer, Julius Boros, Tony Lema, Billy Casper, Gene Littler, Ken Venturi, and Don January) sign it. Years later I'd see that on Byron's mantle and I'd think, Man, that's the nicest thing.

In 1945 there wasn't the clamor there is today. Nobody bothered Byron. He drove to the next tournament, so he was alone then; he could eat dinner and no one would bother him. No TV, no radio. Forget it, just a reporter once and a while. With all the buildup there is now, I don't think Byron could do it again.

He told me he never hit more than a dozen balls before a round. He knew he had it. The only bad thing that could happen to him was if the tournament got rained out.

Golf fans were certainly surprised at what he did that year, but [Jimmy] Demaret, Snead— all the guys he played against—were stunned. I would say it was impossible to win eleven straight tournaments—if he hadn't done it.

—DAVE MARR

- 38 -

Tournament Record 1937

Los Angeles Open - (71) -
1, - 9 - 11 - 37
73 - 71 - 70 - 71 - 285
tied 9th - won "75."

Oakland Open - 68 -
1, - 15 - 17 - 37
75 - 70 - 66 - 73 - 284
tied 17th.

Sacramento Open 72
1, - 22 - 24, 37
69 - 75 - 70 - 71 - 287
6th won $140."

San Francisco Open 71
1, 27 - 31, 37
69 - 70 - 139
Qualified 7th. Beat S. Snead
2-1. Lost to H. Picard 3-2
won $150.00

BOLD AT AUGUSTA

Going into the last nine holes of the 1937 Masters, I was three shots behind Ralph Guldahl. He birdied the tenth, but then so did I, playing in the group behind him. We both parred eleven. But at the par-three twelfth, he hit his ball into the water and made a five. I followed with a birdie at twelve, evening the match.

At the par-five thirteenth, Ralph hit his second shot into Rae's Creek in front of the green and ended up with a bogey six as I watched back in the fairway after hitting my drive to the right slope. Well, I had a three-wood to the green and decided to go for it, even with a breeze against me. I was even with Ralph and knew I had a chance to make a birdie—or better—to increase my lead another stroke or two.

The Lord hates a coward, so I took my wood and made a wonderful shot, knocking it just off to the left side of the green. The flagstick was only about fifteen to eighteen feet away and I chipped

Houston Open 2-12-14-31

Por 71

70-73-74-68- 285

tied 4th. won $250.00

Thomasville 2-19-20-21-31

76-73-70-73- 292-72

tied 14th won $32.00

St. Petersburg 24-26-37

71-69-74-77- 291 -72

won $15.00 tied 14th.

Belleaire 27-28-37

73-70- 72-74- 289

tied 2nd won $400.00

~~Hollywood Ile. 35.~~
~~-277~~ 72

in for an eagle three. That completed a stretch of three, four, two, three—four under par for four holes—and gave me a three-shot lead. I three-putted the par-five fifteenth hole for a par, but still shot a back-nine 32 and ended up winning by two shots over Guldahl.

I'm not saying I was always as bold as I was at thirteen in the final round of the 1937 Masters. You have to play the way you feel. I've seen people go for a shot that I wouldn't have and it worked great. But you have to play your own game. Each shot calls for something different.

MATCH PLAY

Augusta's final-day back nine that year with Guldahl in front of me and us battling it out for the Masters title was almost like match play. We had a lot more match-play tournaments in those days. It would be impractical today to have match play, not only because it is a format that would be

Hollywood Fla.
    Mar. 3-4-5 —   70
68-71-70-68 - 277
tied 5th won $200.00

    Four Ball -
        Mar. 7-
Lost to Metz + Laffoon 2-1
were 16 under for 35 holes

    St. Augustine Pro-Am.
Beat Revolta first round top
lost to Cooper 3-2
won $50.00

    North + South   72
        Mar. 23-25
68-71- 78-75- 292
won 3rd won $500.00

difficult—and risky—to televise, but also because it would be hard for spectators. Tens of thousands of spectators come out each day for tournaments. Having a two-man final match on Sunday would be nearly impossible in terms of crowds. There wouldn't be enough room for them on each hole at one time.

One of my most memorable match-play matches was against Lawson Little at the San Francisco Match Play tournament in 1935. Little, then, was a much-heralded amateur—the best in the world—and I was a relative unknown, paired against him in the first round. I was pretty nervous before the round, but an older pro, Leo Diegel, told me, "Kid, when you get on the first tee, it will be his honor. You will be scared, but just tee it up and hit it as hard as you can. Little doesn't like to be outdriven."

Little hit it good and solid into the fairway, although he didn't really jump on it. It was very wet and his ball didn't roll. My drive carried over where his had stuck. I birdied the hole to his par

Augusta – H – 1 – 4 – 37
66 – 72 – 75 – 70 – 283
Won by # 2 strokes
11   1,500.⁰⁰

Qualifying Nat'l P.G.A
74 – 71 –   145

Nat'l. P.G.A.
May 24 – 30 – 1937
68 – 71 – 139
Medalist by 4 strokes
Beat Diegel   2 – 1
"   Farrell   5 – 4
"   Wood   3 – 2
Lost to Laffron 2 up
won   # 200.⁰⁰

and went on to beat him, five and four.

I had thought of myself as an underdog and won. My theory about match play is that the better player really has to be on his game, especially when playing somebody he hardly knows. You basically have to play the course and not your opponent. But if your opponent hits into trouble—say into the water—you want to make sure you hit it safely to the other side.

Qualifying Natl Open.
70 - 70 - 140

Natl. Open
6 - 10 - 12 -
73 - 78 - 71 - 73 - 295
tied 17th place
won $50.00

British Open
7 - 4 - 9 - 37
75 - 76 - 71 - 74 - 296
was 5th.
won $125.00

Central Penna.
69 - 71 - 140 tie
68 - Play off
won 150.00

Hershey Open

306

Belmont Open
Qualified 141
won tournament $2500.00
Levinson 1 up 19
Walsh 1 up
Mongrum 2 up
Lacey 6-4
Cooper 6-4
Picard 5-4

Miami Biltmore

125.00

Nassau 475.0

Winnings Per Tournament 1937

L.A.	75.00
Oakland	00.00
Sacromento	140.00
San Frimo	150.00
Houston	250.00
Thomasville	32.00
St. Pete	15.00
Belleaire	400.00
Hollywood	200.00
Four Ball	— —
St. Augustine	50.00
Pinehurst	500.00 1813.00
Augusta	1,500.00
P.G.A.	200.00
Nat'l Open	50.00
British "	125.00
Central, Pa.	150.00
Hershey	
Belmont	2500.00
	125.00
Biltmore	47.50
Nassau	

Caddy Fee

$1586.50	$25.50
25.00	10.00
20.00	5.00
18.00	5.00
11.00	5.00
23.50	3.00
11.00	5.00
16.25	5.00
25.50	5.00
17.50	5.00
12.00	5.00
16.00	5.00
30.00	5.00
75.00	5.00
25.00	5.00
27.50	5.00
31.00	5.00
25.00	5.00
32.00	5.00
100.01	10.00
17.50	15.00
18.25	7.50

1937

- 50 -

1938

Byron Nelson? You just said the magic words. When I was a kid, I watched him win the San Francisco Open at Olympic Club in 1944 and 1946. When I got home, I said "Mom, I want to be like Byron Nelson. He's the nicest man; he spoke to me today."

"Well, what did he say?" my mother asked.

He said "Son, would you back up please with your camera and get back behind the ropes."

The punchline is that I dropped that camera off my bike on the way home and ruined the film. How I wish I had those pictures now.

I first met him in 1952. I was playing in the U.S. Amateur at Seattle Golf Club and

Byron watched me with Eddie Lowery [Lowery, a major background figure in the world of golf, was Venturi's employer at a San Francisco car dealership]. I was three down with four to play; I birdied fifteen, sixteen, and seventeen, but my opponent birdied eighteen to win. Byron said "You looked pretty good out there. How would you like to work with me?"

We went down to San Francisco and I took the first formal lesson of my life—from Byron Nelson!

*To me, whatever Byron Nelson said or did was the thing to do, from wearing a coat and tie to how to swing a golf club. My knowledge of the swing is from Byron. His technique was a little different. He kept the club on the ball longer than anyone else in history, because he kept the club **on line** longer than anyone else. As a result, he had that dip in his swing, which was a little hard for me to do. And I could never get my hands as high as Byron's.*

— 1938 —

Los Angeles Open
-77-292

Del Mar Pro-Am-
Crosby tournament
80 - 76 - 156

Pasadena
73 - 71 - 64 - 71 - 279
was 3rd won $350.

He was an excellent chipper and putter, not that it was a very aesthetic-looking stroke, not like Ben Crenshaw's. It was very firm, very decisive. His stroke said, "You're going in."

Yes, some people think he retired too early (at the end of 1946), but after the 1945 he had, Byron was the epitome of "What else is there for me to do?"

—KEN VENTURI

GOLFING IN THE WIND

There wasn't a whole lot to talk about in 1938. I played in twenty-five tournaments and won two. I played well in a few others, but for the most part my game wasn't to the level I would have preferred.

One of the few things that sticks out from 1938 was the San Francisco Match Play tournament early in the year. The wind was really kicking up. In fact, hurricane warnings had been posted along the bay. But we played on. I shot a

Oakland, Calif.
75-71-71-79-296

Sacramento
75-75-74-70-294
8th won $100.

San Francisco
Match Play
82-76-158
Lost Paul Runyon 1st match
Second Driving Contest
204-207-221- 632
won 75⁰⁰ 35⁰⁰ $110.⁰⁰

first-round 77 to lead all qualifiers, which says something about how bad the wind was.

The assumption is that you have to hit the ball low to be a good bad-weather player. But that's not the secret to it. Sure, sometimes you have to keep it down when you're playing a shot to the green. What is most important is hitting the ball *solidly*. A lot of people playing in the wind will swing harder, trying to hit the ball harder. Their timing gets off and they don't make good contact. Therefore, the ball doesn't go as far as you want it to.

Jimmy Demaret was a wonderful wind player. I played well in the wind and there were a few others. They all concentrate on one thing—hitting the ball solidly. Keep your rhythm, try to hold your balance, and brace yourself against the wind. Maybe widen your stance a little bit. As tall as he is, George Archer is able to play well in the wind because he compensates by bending his knees a little more than most people, thus lowering his center of gravity to help stabilize him in the wind.

New Orleans La.
   Feb. 20·21·22
79·77·77· 73· 306

Thomasville Ga.
  25·26·27 - Feb.
66. 73 - 71- 70· 280
won by 4 stroke
     $700.00

St. Petersburg.
  Mar 2-3-4-
72-71-69-71- 283
third one stroke back.
won $350.00

Hollywood, Fla.
  Mar 9-10-11
72-71- 69- 71- 283
won back.-   350.00

Hollywood – Mar.
71 · 68 · 69 – 67 – 275
won 1st and $700.⁰⁰

Int. Four Ball
Beat Farrell + Klein 2-1
Beat Shute + Moore 2-1
Lost Loffoon + Metz 3-2
won $150.⁰⁰

Pinehurst N C
69 – 72 – 71 – 74 – 286
Tied 3rd won $400.⁰⁰

Greensboro N C
80 – 71 – 75 – 70 – 296

Augusta. Ga. 1-4-
74 – 73 – 70 – 73 – 290
5th won $400⁰⁰

June.   3-5 -
K. C. Open
picks up

June   9-11 -
Nat'l Open
77-71-74-72 - 294
won 5th + 412.50
P. G. a.
July 10-16
Qualified 14 @
Beat Yockey   5-4
"   Kruger 1 up 20
"   Gossler 11-4 @ -shot 64
new course record
Lost to Hines 2-1
Won $250.00
Central Penna Open
66 - 75 - 141
second $90.00

Sept. 1 - 4.
 Hershey Open
won $325.00
  + 0
New York "108"
 Sept. 24 - 27
72 - 76 - 75 - 71 - 69 - 71 - 434
tied 2nd. won 900.00

Columbia, S.C.

75 - 73 - 72 - 73 -
 - 293 -
Augusta Open
73 - 72 - 70 - 73
 - 288 -

- 60 -

$
10,000

Miami Open
77 - 76 - 153
failed to qualify

Houston
77 - 75 - 67 = 219
tied 5th won $1,86.⁶⁶

Cleveland

$
100.⁰⁰

"1938"

Tournament Winnings

Los Angeles	—
Crosby	—
Pasadena	350.00
Oakland	—
Sacramento	100.00
San Frisco	110.00
New Orleans	—
Thomasville	700.00
St. Pete	350.00
Hollywood	700.00
Four Ball	150.00
Pinehurst	400.00
Greensboro	—
Augusta	400.00
K.C.	—
Nat'l Open	412.50
P.G.A.	250.00
C.P.O.	90.00
Cleve	100.00

"1938"

Hershey	325.00
New York	900.00
Columbia	—
Augusta	—
Memphis	—
Houston	186.66
25	8 5,524 16

Caddy Fee	Intro Fee
17.50	5.00
12.00	3.00
25.00	5.00
13.00	5.00
12.00	5.00
16.00	5.00
14.00	5.00
75.00	5.00
40.00	5.00
75.00	5.00
25.00	5.00
22.50	5.00
12.00	6.00
31.00	6.00
22.50	5.00
42.00	5.00
21.00	5.00
10.00	5.00
7.50	

"1938"

Caddy Fee	Entry Fee
43.00	12.50
18.00	5.00
26.00	5.00
25.00	10.00
16.00	5.00
21.00	5.00
646.00	132.50

1939

Byron had that rocking motion in his swing which was so distinctive and so effective. I think timing is in your feet a lot, so that's where his tremendous rhythm and timing came from. And with that big lateral move, he was able to create a longer "flat spot;" he simply kept the club on line longer than anybody else.

I first met him in the late forties when he and Jug McSpaden came to our course [Wichita Country Club in Kansas] to play an exhibition. I just marveled at how straight he was and at how he could shoot a 72 on a golf course he'd never seen before. It was obvious to me even then that he was a very considerate, gentle man.

Tournaments for "1939"

L. A. Open
72-70-74-70- 286
tied 7th won $129.25

Oakland
72-69-70-69- 280
won 8th won $230.00

Fresno Match Play
74-69- 143
Lost 1st round to Coltrin 2-1
75.00

Exhibition Santa Barbara
shot 70 - $100.00

Crosby Pro-am
68-71- 139
tied 2nd won $300.00

He proved how nice he was again in 1957, when he and Ben Hogan played with me and Barbara Romack in the Pro-Am before the [LPGA] Civitan Open in Dallas. Not all the men pros supported or encouraged the women, but those two did, and we loved them for it. Then in 1987, at the first Marilynn Smith Founders tournament (for senior women professionals), Byron and Peggy came and handed out the prizes to the winning pro-am teams. For all his help, I have a soft spot in my heart for Byron Nelson.

—MARILYNN SMITH

CADDIES

Caddies didn't travel with the golfers back in those days because you couldn't pay them enough to cover their travel expenses. Every place you went, you had a new caddie. They would assign you a caddie when you got there. If you went back to

Texas Open

67-69--69 69-274
won 3rd won $550.00

Phoenix Open

68-65-65-198
1st by 12 strokes - $700.00

Pro-am - 64-   26.65

New Orleans

74-73-69-75-291
tied 5th won $350.00

Pro-am. 64- ..   62.50

Thomasville

72-74-69- 215
tied 4th won
            $183.34

the same place for a tournament, you just might pick up the same caddie. That was the only time you had a familiar face working for you.

Today caddies know almost as much about the game as the golfers do. Not fully, but they know your swing and can tell you when your tempo is a little off. The game is more sophisticated now. Caddies make a lot of money and they're well-trained—just like the old Scottish caddies who could tell you what club to use and how to use it.

Ben Hogan used to ask a caddie: Do you know the rules? It has always been important for caddies to know the rules. In those days, for example, there was a rule that you couldn't hit the flagstick with your shot when your ball was within sixty feet of the hole—unless you were in a hazard. This meant someone had to be tending the flagstick, even if you were off the green in the fairway or the rough. If the caddie could convince Ben that he knew the rules, Ben would just say, "Okay, just carry my bag and keep quiet."

St. Petersburg
70-7/- 70 - 211
Tied 4th   250.00

Four Ball
Lost to Harrison - Morgan
    won $50.00

Seminole   Inv.
68 - won $565.00+

Indian Creek
73 - won $25.00+

St. Augustine

Best Ball ~~2-1~~ 1 up
  " Smith 2-1
Lost Stahl 2-1
won $75.00

The only place I ever had the same caddie was Augusta. They had the same caddies there for years. I had a young man named Shotgun who caddied for me. In my entire career, I never asked a caddie what club to use. I always knew what to use. Judgment of distance is a skill.

1939 PGA CHAMPIONSHIP

*T*he funny part about our match in the finals of the 1939 PGA [at Pomonok Country Club, Long Island, New York] was on the first tee in the morning round. Byron swung and almost missed the ball entirely; I don't know if you should write that, because it was so unlike him. The ball went way off to the right into the bushes, so I started the match one-up.

North + South
    Pinehurst
71-68-70-71-280
won by 2 strokes
    $1,000.00

    Greensboro
73-73-70-74-290
10th - won $170.00

    Augusta

71-69-72-75-287
was 7th. won
    $250.00
Natl. Open - Phila
73-72-71-68-284
Tied. wood - Shute
    "   "   68-68
won   70-73

Twice during the round he chipped in over my ball for birdies, and I missed both my putts. But the key hole was number nine in the afternoon round, when he made a great shot from the trees onto the green and we halved the hole with pars.

Byron was one-up coming to the last hole. I had nothing to lose, so I hit my driver as hard and as far as I could, about fifty to one hundred dred yards ahead of him. Byron hit it on the green to within five feet of the hole and I hit a wedge to about two feet.

"Byron," I said, "I'm sorry, but I just laid you a dead stymie." *[Picard's ball blocked Nelson's path to the hole; the match play rules then in effect did not require the competitors to mark their balls].* Well, Byron hit the most beautiful putt I've ever seen, **around** my ball and almost in the hole. Then I banked my ball in off his for a birdie.

Open &
won   1 0 0 0.⁰⁰

Inverness In.
Plus 6 - tied
lost 1st hole
won   4 / 2.⁵⁰

Mass. State Open
70-71-71-71- 283

won by 4 strokes
"   400.⁰⁰
*25⁰ appearance
Scranton Open

35.⁰⁰

On the first hole of sudden death, a sound truck ran over my ball in the right rough [this was the first golf tournament ever broadcast on radio]. I got a free drop and got it on the green, about fifteen feet, and was lucky enough to make it. Byron had hit his iron shot to five feet.

"Anyone like to putt this for me?" he said.

"Well, I would," I said.

He missed, so I won. Oh yes, he was very gracious about it. A gentleman.

Did you know he was the youngest-ever winner of the Masters? [Jack Nicklaus broke Nelson's age record in winning the 1963 Masters.]

And he was the greatest putter God ever put on the Earth. And the best iron player and... he was just a helluva good golfer.

—HENRY PICARD

I feel very privileged in having his friendship. I've talked about Byron Nelson all over the U.S. and I've never met anybody

P. G. A.

Beat chuck Garringer
" Red Francis
" John Revolta
" Kimericks, cousin
" Dutch Harrison
lost to Picard on 37th
won 600.00

western open
68-7? - 70-7/- 281
won by 1 stroke
won 7 - 0.00
Special Prize 60.00

St. Paul
68-73-66-74 - 281
tied 10 th won 205.00
200.00 appearance money

he's (ticked) off. And he was always so support-
ive of us when we were kids. Not that he's
Mister Goody Two-Shoes—that doesn't describe
him. Let me tell you a couple of war stories:

In college [at North Texas State] in about
1955, I went on a three-day exhibition with
him to Louisiana while the rest of the team went
to a tournament in Mexico City. When we
came back, the USGA [United States Golf
Association] said everybody on the team had lost
his amateur status for accepting expense money.
Right away Byron wrote some letters, made
some calls, and got us reinstated. Without
Byron, we wouldn't have cracked the code.

In the last of those exhibitions in Louisiana,
Byron had the shanks something awful. Must
have shanked thirty. But bless his heart, he was
a gentleman about it. On the trip back home in
his Lincoln, I finally got up the courage to ask
him: "Pro (I always called him Pro, never
Byron), you had a hard day today. Had you
ever shanked a golf ball before?" And he said,

Ofsen Dar
        Pittsburg. Pa
72-71-73. 75. 291
    tied 7th. won 39%. 66

    Central, Pa. open
    68-69. 137
    won -   100 - x

    Burkshire, Pro. Am.
    66- 68 -134 - 100
    68 - 69 - 137   40
    won   x 140

        Chicago
    Hagen 25 ammimary
+ H was 3rd
    won $ 400.00

- 79 -

"Yes, I usually shanked once every seventy-two-hole tournament."

Another time, Billy Maxwell and I played Byron in the Texas Cup Match [amateurs vs. professionals] at Dallas Country Club. Well, we caught lightning in a bottle and beat them, seven and six. Sometimes when you get your head stuffed between your legs you get belligerent, but again Byron was very gracious and complimentary.

The courses in the forties weren't as long, but the greens weren't as good, either; the greens weren't as good as the fairways are now. And I don't care if some of the players were in the service or overseas—the secret to the whole thing was his scoring average. What was it, 68.3? You couldn't do that if they gave you all your ten-foot putts.

—DON JANUARY

Ryder cup match at Dallas

McSpaden - Nelson won 2 ½
in Scotch forssome against
Irold and Barnum

Nelson Thomson won 4 - 3
in four ball. Shot 66 for low
round of Day. won
$40.00

Four Ball - Miami
Beat Farrell - Dudley - 6 - 4
lost to Smith Runyan - 5 - 4
Won $ 75.00

Seminole $ 20.00
Indian Creek   2500
Thomasville, Ga.
68 - 68 - 69 - 205
2nd won   4 5 0 . 0 0

Hershey

68 - 73 - 71 - 75 - 287

was 4th. won *450.00

Gift on last ball - $300.00

750.00

Phila. P.G.A. "Medal Champ"

69 - 68 - 137.

won 1st and $100.00

Miami Open

68 · 69 · 68 · 73 · 278.

was 5th won $600.00

Totals 1939 $11,235.90

12.00	5.00
25.50	5
14.00	5
30.00	5
40.00	5
22.50	5
18.00	10
16.00	8
14.00	5
12.50	5
9.00	5
50.00	
12.00	5
21.00	5
169.00	5
10.00	
40.00	5
22.50	5
50.00	5
20.00	750

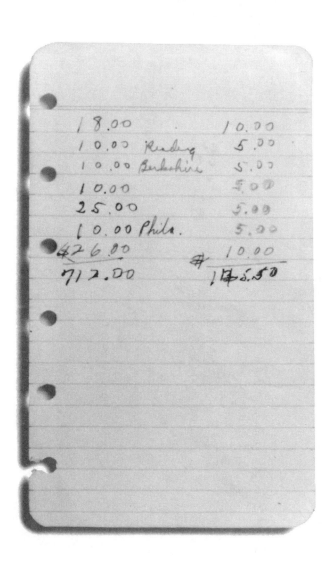

18.00		10.00
10.00	Reading	5.00
10.00	Berkshire	5.00
10.00		5.00
25.00		5.00
10.00	Phila.	5.00
676.00		10.00
712.00		175.50

1940

You know, I never did play that much with Byron, in tournaments or in practice rounds. I think he quit a little too early. He would have won more...He was a helluva player and a real nice guy, too.

We played head-to-head four times. He won two and I won two...The key hole in one of those match-es, our PGA final [at Hershey Country Club in Pennsylvania] in 1940, was number eight. The green was down in a hol-

low and it didn't get much sun. I hit my ball on the green about six feet from the hole in two and Byron made a bogey five. Do you know I never did get my ball in the hole? Some dirt was stuck *on it and it wouldn't roll any way but side-ways, and of course you couldn't clean your ball in those days. So Byron won the hole with a bogey and he won the match one-up.*

Byron hit the ball so straight, but you know one time he said to me "I wish I could hit against my left side like you." Well, different swings for different people.

*Byron didn't smoke, didn't drink, didn't play around, didn't dance and I wondered just what the hell **does** he do?*

—SAM SNEAD

MORE ON PRACTICE

Let's go back to my earlier comments regarding practice. I made a brief reference to the 1940 Texas Open at Brackenridge Park in San Antonio, where I ended up in a playoff with Ben Hogan. After the regulation seventy-two holes and before the play-off, Ben and I were interviewed by a San Antonio

Tournaments "1940"

L. A. Open
74 - sick Flu.

Oakland
Flu

San Francisco
Qualified 71 - 73 - 144
Beat Red Fransin   2 - 1
  " Chas. Klien   4 - 3
Lost to Goggin   4 - 2
won $150.00

Crosby
74 - NC

Phoenix
74 - 73 - 68 -   215
no end

radio station. I said my piece and then Ben was asked about being in a playoff with me. He answered, Byron's got a good game, but it'd be a lot better if he'd practice. He's too lazy to practice.

Well, I guess I could end this story just by saying that I went out and beat Ben in the next day's eighteen-hole playoff, 70 to 71. But he was right, except for the part about my being lazy. I didn't practice much, but that was by design. I had my swing pretty well groomed—and grooved. It didn't make sense to me to be going out to the range and beating several hundred balls a day. To each his own.

Golf is like anything else. You learn by doing. Whether it's eating, walking, or driving a car, you just keep doing it until you can do it subconsciously. It takes some people longer than others to learn how to do it automatically. That's why in golf some people need to practice more than others.

I think Ben practiced more than anybody I ever saw. Not that he hit six hundred balls a day like some of today's players do. But Ben would go

J ups Ofen
68-67-69-67- 271
Lind Hogan
won play off 70 to 71
won 11 2 5
extra gate 2 1 1 83

Houston - Western
78 - finish ups
Financed
New Orleans
74-73-78- 70- 295
14 th won $146.00

St. Petersburg

· 71-72-69- 212
2nd won $450.00

through a couple buckets of balls a day. I saw Johnny Revolta, who was a wonderful player and who won the PGA Championship (in 1935), practice until he would get these big calluses on his hands. He had dry skin, so he would use this razor-type thing to cut the calluses off, then would get right back to practicing. I understand that baseball pitcher Nolan Ryan used to do the same thing with his pitching hand—shave off skin calluses so that he could grip the ball better.

I never did practice much. If I had, maybe I would have been better. Then again, I might not have been as good had I practiced more.

Several years ago, I went to the PGA awards dinner to accept an award on behalf of the GTE Byron Nelson Classic, and Peggy and I ended up sitting at a table that also included Lee Trevino and his wife, and Greg Norman and his wife. In the course of conversation while eating, Greg asked me how much I practiced when I played. I told him that I had hardly practiced at all after I learned to play the way I wanted to play. Oh sure,

North + South - Pinehurst
70-73-74-70. 286
3rd won $500.00

Greensboro NC
73-71-68-68. 280
tied 3rd. won $412.50

Ashville N C
67-74-71-72- 284
won 7th - $230.00

Augusta Ga
69-72-74-70. 285
3rd won $600.00

Ohio State open
72-69-72-71- 284
won 1st rd $250.00

I practiced a few shots to warm up and get the feel of the sand and rough, but I didn't just go out and beat balls. After my first two or three years, I never practiced *after* a round.

This awards dinner was right after Lee had had a sensational year in his first year on the senior tour, winning something like eight tournaments. After I finished explaining to Greg my hands-off philosophy of practice, Lee jumped in and said, "Greg, I hit some balls to warm up and practiced a little bit this year, but I never hit a ball after I played a round in that entire year, either."

Greg couldn't believe it. Practice is a personal thing, although you do have to practice when you're learning to play.

THE HOGAN WAY

Ben Hogan practiced a lot because it was hard for Ben to learn how to play. Once he learned how to play, he played great! The reason he played great is

Goodall Round Robin
6th and won $375.00

Natl Open

73 - 78 - 70 - 74 - 290
Tied 5th - won $325.00

Inverness Invitational
Finish tie for last - 14
won $175.00

P. G. A

won $2,100.00

because he worked at it very, very hard. He learned to concentrate that way.

The talk over the years has been about Ben being cold on the golf course and not talking to anybody. That is what he had to do to concentrate. If he broke his concentration, it took him two or three holes to get back into his concentration zone.

As for me, yeah, I talked a lot, especially if I was playing well. I always talked.

Swinging in the Rain

We talked earlier in the book about playing in windy conditions. Now let's talk about playing golf in another form of inclement weather, namely the rain. Unless it's really raining hard or there's lightning in the area, tournament officials will allow play to continue. That's why it's important for a golfer to know how to adjust to wet play. It takes more than just knowing how to open the

Scranton

271

2nd run 750.⁰⁰

Miami, Fla. Open
69-65-67-70-271
won and $2,537.⁵⁰

~~1940~~
~~won - 9,670.33~~
1940
won # 9,696.⁰⁰

umbrella; you also need to be prepared to keep your grips dry and to adjust your club selection accordingly.

Rain played a big part in the 1940 North and South Open at Pinehurst in North Carolina. The rain got pretty bad during the last day. I didn't handle it well and had a terrible last round, shooting a 76 to tie for fourth place. I didn't play in glasses then, and I feel sorry for people that have to wear glasses and are playing in the rain.

The thing about playing in the rain is that you have to be careful *not* to overswing. Play a little shorter, a little firmer, and use a little more club. Remember, the ball going through the air is being hit by water. It's simple: The harder it's raining, the more the ball is being hit, and therefore it is being slowed and knocked down. Adjust accordingly.

In those days, we would keep playing, even in the hard rain—at least until the hole was under water. When faced with puddles near or on the green, you either had to lay up around it or chip over it. Today, it's a different game out there.

Caddy & Entry Fee
1940

10.00	5.00
12.00	5.00
14.00	8.00
15.00	5.00
50.00	5.00
6.00	5.00
16.00	10.00
25.00	5.00
5.00	5.00
12.00	5.00
2.00	5.00
2.50	5.00
2 2.50	
30.00	5.00
3 0.00	5.00
20.00	5.00
30.00	5.00
40.00	5.00
15.00	5.00
14.00	5.00
18.00	X
35.50	

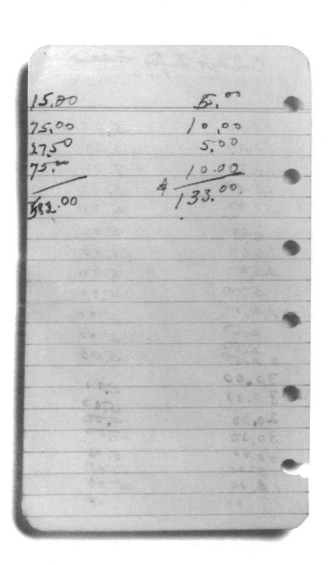

15.00	5.00
75.00	10.00
27.50	5.00
75.00	10.00
582.00	$ 133.00

1941

Byron's such a strong man; the club looks like a toothpick in his hands. But though his hands are very strong, they're very soft. He held them firmly on the golf club, but he did not allow them to overpower his swing. Meanwhile, his lower body kept the club-face square to the target line. He **never** hit a wild slice or a swinging hook, like I do on occasion.

My father was a golf historian of sorts and he liked to talk to me when I was a kid about the records of the great players. "Never to be

equaled" was the phrase he used about what Byron did in 1945. And I remember him saying Nelson won nineteen tournaments that year, not eighteen [Watson's father was correct, but Nelson's nineteenth was unofficial, because the purse in the Spring Lake event was only twenty-five hundred dollars; official tournaments had to have prize money of at least three thousand dollars].

His advice to me was always very simple and very positive...When I won the British Open at Carnoustie in '75, it had been nice all week until the final round, and the wind really started to blow.

"It's a different course today," he told me. "If you stay around par you will have a good chance."

Well, I did stay around par [actually one under par] and I won in a playoff the next day with Jack Newton. Byron was right again.

Winning the Nelson four times was obviously wonderful because of my relationship with

1941

Entry Fee		Caddy Fees
5.00	L.A.	23.00
5.00	Okl	19.00
5.00	Frisco	20.00
5.00	Crosby	21.00
5.00	Phoenix	35.00
5.00	Lexow	25.00
5.00	U.O.	17.50
5.00	Thomasville	12.50
5.00	St. Pete	19.00
5.00	Four Balls	12.00
	Simile	40.00
5.00	Bel air	40.00
5.00	Pinehurt	20.00
5.00	W. Salm	17.00
5.00	Greensboro	75.00
5.00	Ashville	20.00
5.00	Masters	50.00
5.00	Nat'l	40.00
5.00	R.G.A.	70.00
90.00		576.00

Byron and Louise. . .But I didn't enjoy the vic-
tories because I always wanted more. (Then)
Byron gave me his most enduring advice: It's not
how you play, it's how you conduct yourself and
how you treat people.

—TOM WATSON

Sportsmanship

Perhaps more than any other sport, golf remains a game of etiquette and sportsmanship. Golfers are expected to abide by a traditional set of rules and that sometimes means either accepting a strange ruling that works against you or calling a penalty on yourself, even when no one else has witnessed the indiscretion. That's why they say golf truly is a game of character.

One of my most memorable tests of character occurred at the 1941 PGA Championship at Cherry Hills Country Club in Denver. Talk about surviving a gauntlet of great players: To get to the

1941

Rob... ... Caddy Fee

           →   Thurman   35.00

7.50   St. Paul   25.00

5.00   Toledo   10.00

5.00   Detroit P.G.A.   12.00

5.00   Ohio Open   20.00

11.00   Chicago   100.00

5.00   Hurst   30.00

~~5.00~~   ~~L.P.G.A.~~ ~~10.00~~

10.00   Miami   95.00

5.00   Harlingen 20.00

5.00   Beaumont 22.00

58.50   369.00

90.00   576.00

148.50   Total   945.00

match-play finals, I had to beat the likes of Bill Heinlein, Ralph Guldahl, Ben Hogan, and Gene Sarazen—to get a crack at Vic Ghezzi, a wonderful player.

Against Vic, I was leading three-up with nine holes to go in the thirty-six-hole match, when the adrenaline just flowed out of my body. I didn't have any gas left in the tank and it showed. Vic caught me at the end of regulation, forcing a sudden-death playoff.

On the second playoff hole, we both hit our chips about four feet past the hole. Mine was about a half-inch farther away, with Vic's ball resting about eight inches to the left of mine. The referee asked me if Vic's ball was in my way. I said no and then took my stance. Inadvertently, I nudged Vic's ball with my foot, moving it about an inch.

Such a violation means loss of hole in match play and I conceded, although Vic wouldn't accept winning that way and told me to go ahead and putt. The official concurred. But I knew I had lost by the rules and lacking any semblance of

Phoenix - Western Open
68 - 69 - 67 - 74 - 278
tied 3rd
won $600.⁰⁰

Texas Open
71 - 71 - 69 - 71 - 282
tied 5th won $325.⁰⁰

New Orleans Open
75 - 69 - 69 - 72 - 285
tied 8th won 210.⁰⁰

Thomasville Open

$1875⁰⁰

concentration, I missed the putt and lost the match. I did not miss the putt on purpose. I knew if I made the putt and Vic missed his, I would win and everything would have broken loose. I lost that match two ways: by letting down like I did and by moving that ball.

There is no other sport like golf. That's why golf is so great—because of the rules and in the way the players conduct themselves. Today, players will inform other competitors of a rules violation *before* they sign the scorecard rather than waiting until after the scorecard is signed, which would lead to disqualification.

I have called things on myself when no one else saw it. One time at the British Open, the wind blew my ball while I was addressing it and it rolled over. There wasn't television in those days where viewers at home pick out penalties. But that didn't matter. I never hesitated calling the penalty on myself.

I lost the 1946 U.S. Open largely because of some of the worst luck in the world: On the

St. Petersburg

74 -   - 65 - 77

tied last - won $40.⁰⁰

Miami - Fri.m Ball
Lost to Smith & Runyan - 1 down
on 38 - won $15.⁰⁰

Seminole -

64 - Pro - Amateur 70 & S.
Won 232.⁵⁰
Partner $71.79
$803.29

Belleair - Fla.
72 - 67 - 67 - 206
tied Smith
68 - 69 Lost to Smith
won $500.⁰⁰

thirteenth hole of the third round, my caddie accidentally kicked my ball resting on the fairway. It wasn't his fault, though. It was on a par-five hole. There was a marshal standing along the fairway, holding a rope that he would pull up after players hit their second shots, allowing the gallery to cross the fairway behind the second-shot landing area. I knew I couldn't reach the green with my second shot, so I laid it up back in the fairway a little bit, within a few feet of the spectators.

My caddie was behind me as we walked under the rope held up by the marshal. The caddie had his head down going under the rope and didn't see the ball, thinking it was another ten to fifteen feet ahead. He kicked it, costing me a penalty stroke. I had been playing like gangbusters up until then, but was two over par the rest of the round and ended up in a tie at the end of regulation the next day with Lloyd Mangrum and Vic Ghezzi, only to lose in a second playoff. It's all just part of the game.

Pinehurst, N.C.
69 - 71 - 69 - 76 - 285
tied for 4th. won $350.00

Winston-Salem Pro-Am.
65 + 71 won $133.33

Greensboro - N.C.
72 - 64 - 70 - 70 - 276
won by 2 strokes
won $1200.00

Ashville, N.C.

10th won $155-00
Augusta National
71 - 69 - 73 - 70 - 283
2nd - won $800.00

Nat'l Open

73 - 73 - 74 - 77 - 297
won   50 ⁰⁰

P. G. A.
Beat Tinfay   - Bros.
  "   Hemlien   2 up
  "   Guldahl   2 - 1
  "   Hagen   2 up
  "   Sarazen   2 - 1
Lost Gharris   on   3 8
                6 00 ⁰⁰
Inavass Invitational
won   6 00 ⁰⁰

St. Paul
tied 5th   28/won 277 ⁵⁰

Toledo District
71 - 6 8 - 137 9
won   75 ⁰⁰

G.P.d.

69 - won

100.00

Chicago open

67 - 69 - 72 - 10 - 278
won $2000.00

Hurst Invitational
71 - 72 - 74 - 68 - 285
fin'd 6th won $350.00

Ohio Open
68 - 69 - 72 - 62 - 271
won 1st $125.00

Miami Open
70 - 67 - 66 - 66 - 269
won - $2537.50

- III -

Harlinger Texas
70-65-70-66- 271
4 th won   450.00

Beaumont open
71-69-74-72-286
tied 7 th won $225.00

1941

won 11,819,12

      2 7 tournaments

1942-43

Byron Nelson was the first golf professional I ever saw, when he and Jug
McSpaden played an exhibition at our
course, San Diego Country Club, in 1946.
Oh, I thought, he was beauti-
ful...such grace. I decided right
then that professional golf was
what I wanted to do.

To me, he was always the pic-
ture of a golf swing. When I was
fifteen or sixteen, you could really
see I was imitating him. I had that
upright swing and I dropped into
the ball, although I worked to get
rid of that drop later. My teacher told me that
Byron had the first one-piece takeaway from the
ball—the first modern swing. The oldtimers like
Sarazen were all hands and wrists. I went to
watch Byron at Dallas Athletic Club when he

*was about fifty and he still had that same, love-
ly swing.*

*What is it like to win a lot of tournaments in
a row? [Wright twice won four consecutive
events]. Exhausting. Being in contention every
week is exhausting, to begin with. Then when
you start winning, the pressure builds so much,
you want to crawl into a hole. So what Byron
did was mind-boggling. Awe inspiring. They try
to put an asterisk by his record, but just look at
some old film of the conditions of the golf courses back then. And look at the scores he shot!*

—MICKEY WRIGHT

HOLDING THE GREENS

Another big difference in today's game versus my
era in the thirties and forties was in the way you
approached the greens with shots. There was no
such thing as backing the ball up with backspin in

1 9 4 2

L. A. Open. 1 - 9 - 13 -
72 - 74 - 70 - 72 - tied 6th
258
tied 6th won $350°°

Oakland 1 - 15 - 18 -
67 - 69 - 69 - *69 - 274
won by batches - 1000°°

San Francisco Open
287

200
Crosby Pro. Am.
70 - 72 - 142.
57°°

Western Open. Phoenix
72 - 68 - 73 - 72 -
tied 11th   285
*105.°°
pro am   4 - 50.°°

those days. We played on a lot of greens that just didn't back up. So even when we came across those rare greens on which it was possible to back the ball up, we weren't accustomed to it. So we didn't do it.

Those greens actually were a little harder at the surface. They cut the bermuda grass right down to the root, then overseeded with rye and a couple other combinations. The greens putted well—they were like glass—but they were really fast and firm. They were every bit as fast as they are now.

You could *hear* your ball on your approach shots land on the green. That's how hard the greens were. You couldn't quite hear it if you were one hundred fifty to two hundred yards back. But if you had a pitch shot, you could hear the ball impact the putting surface. The trick was to play your shots high and soft. I could hit the knock-down shots when I needed them, but I could also make the ball land softly on the green. I was pretty good with a nine-iron.

Texas Open - San Antonio
74-67-73-10
284

won   won/62.⁵⁰
New Orleans Open
74-73-69-71- 287
won 6th won $300.⁰⁰
06 Pro Am won 50.⁰⁰

St. Peter
68-76 75 70 289
tied 2 nd won 5 83.³³

Four Ball
Beatt/Halbert/Byrd 3-2
Lost to Harper+/Heiser/up
won/00.⁰⁰

- 117 -

Hitting those high shots that land softly really paid off for me over the years at Augusta. I think I won in my third trip there. They post a golfer's cumulative score there and after the first two Masters Tournaments, I was in the red and stayed there, covering more than nine hundred holes of Masters play.

Nowadays, golf manufacturers have all different kinds of wedges for hitting those high, soft shots. There is the 60-degree wedge, for instance. If you can reach the green with it, you can stop it.

Seminole Fla.
74 - 72 - 146
won $50⁰⁰

North + South -
69 - 70 - 69 - 73 - 281
tied 3rd won $500⁰⁰

Greensboro NC
72 - 68 - 68 - 74 - 282
tied 4 th - won $412⁵⁰
tied low 3rd round 25.-

Asheville NC

$
200⁰⁰

Augusta Nat'l.
68 - 67 - 73 - 72 - 280
tied Hogan
69 - to 70 Play off #
o. Date   won $1500.⁰¹

I carry three wedges—a 46-degree, a 54-degree, and a 60-degree. That's why some golfers carry only one wood—at least hardly ever more than two—so they can use more of these short irons in their allotment of fourteen clubs in the bag.

DRIVE FOR SHOW

We had a long-driving contest nearly every week. I wasn't considered a long driver, so I usually didn't get in them. But sometimes they would want me to hit, so I was game.

You had to keep it in bounds to win, and while mine wouldn't be real long, I won a few of them that way—just by hitting the ball straight.

THE BABE

One time I was partnered with Babe Didrickson Zaharias in the pro-am of the Beverly Hills Open.

1 9 4 2

Coddy Fee		Entry
55 —	La.	10⁰⁰
37.50	Oaks	5 —
30.⁰⁰	Frisco	5 —
17⁰⁰	Crosby	5 —
32 —	Western Open	5 —
25 —	Sigma Open	5 —
23 .	New Orleans	5 —
25 —	St Pete	5 —
12 —	4 Ball	5 —
8 —	Seminole	—
40 —	Pinehurst	5 —
27 —	Greensboro	5
26 —	Ashville	5
100 —	Augusta	5
15 —	Boston	5
20 —	P.G.A	5
25 —	Inverness	5
22 —	Hale America	5
125 —	Inv Orchanters	12⁵⁰
674.50 Total		102.50

When we got to the first tee that day, without having played a practice round or anything, Babe said, loud enough for everyone to hear, "Well, Byron, you're my partner today, did you know that?"

I said, "Yes, I saw it in the newspaper and I must say I'm pleased."

She said, "So am I. But I want to tell you something They're only giving me four shots from the men's tees. That's not enough, but I can choose those four shots and shoot a 66. If you can help me another four shots, we can win the tournament."

And that's exactly what happened. We shot 62. Babe was amazing. She was the best woman athlete ever.

1942

15.00   Ichito of   5.00

22.50   Ohio of   5.00

712.00   112.50

1944

I got out of the service late in '44 and I was so anxious to get back to the tour. I won the first tournament in Los Angeles, and three in a row a little later (at Gulfport in a playoff with Nelson), and at Pensacola and Jacksonville), but then...then it was Byron's year.

—SAM SNEAD

I first met Byron at Pasadena in '33. I knew he was going to be a fine player, but I was better then; in '33 and '34, I won six straight tournaments. I gave **him** lessons. I had a number of the best women amateur players in the country at Philadelphia Country Club, where I was the pro: Glenna Collett Vare, Dorothy Germain Porter...Byron would call me on the phone when he thought he wasn't

1964

Pro- Amateur
Hillcrest
Par 72 - shot 65
won $125 War Bonds

Pro- Amateur
San Gabriel
Par 71 - shot 67
won - $127.00

L. A. open
283 - Par 284
tied 3rd. won $125. Bonds
68-72-71-72 = 283

San Francisco open
275 - Par - 288
won 1st - won $2,400 Bonds
68-69- 68-70- 275

- 125 -

hitting it straight enough, but I'll tell you, he never left the fairway. The strength of his game? He was a great driver and he was the best two-wood player I ever saw. He'd be twelve-under par on the par-fives every week. People couldn't believe he could play that well.

—JUG MCSPADEN

WHEN THE GOING GETS ROUGH

One of the best lessons I ever gave myself was knowing how to play out of the rough. Even in my playing days, the toughest rough always seemed to pop up at the U.S. Open. The United States Golf Association, which runs the U.S. Open among other prestigious national events, is notorious for growing the rough thick and long for its events. So I had some good practice in learning how to play out of the rough. I believe the lessons learned apply to all golfers today.

1944

Pro. Amateur Phoenix
64 - won $150.00

Phoenix open
71 - 66 - 71 - 65 - 273
Tied - McSpaden
Lost in Playoff - shot 72
won = $1325.00 Bond

Texas open
75 - 63 - 68 - 68 - 274
Tied 2nd won $862.50
Bond

New Orleans open

71 - 78 - 71 - 70 - 290
2nd won $1000.00 Bond

- 127 -

When in the rough, the average player will try to hit the ball harder so as to get it out and over the tough grass. You need to hit the ball harder, yes, but it's also important that you use the right club. Use your own judgment in picking a club that will allow you to quickly get the ball up and out of the grass. A straight-faced club, like a two- or three-iron isn't the best solution. Instead, use a club with some loft, such as a seven-wood or even a five-wood. The point is, get the ball back onto the fairway.

Bad holes are a result of trying to hit a miracle shot out of bad places. Sometimes if you try to do something unusual to get out of the rough, you will miss it. Then you are in even worse shape. Advance the ball out to where you can have a free shot for the next shot and then most of the time you won't make anything worse than a bogey. Also, when in the rough, you have to yank the club out as quickly as possible after striking the ball. Hit down on the ball, then get that club up and out of there.

1944

Gulfport Open
72-71-70-70- 289
was 3rd won $500.00 and
$187.50 cash

Charlotte Open
70-70-73-66- 279
was 3rd won $1000.00 2nd

Charlotte Driving contest
$50.00 2nd

Durham Open
68-67-69-70- 274
2nd won $750.00

Knoxville
69-68-66-67- 270
won 1st $
1,000.00

Jack Nicklaus was the best rough player I ever saw for long shots. He used an upright swing, and really used his legs and had his body coming through. He would come right up with it. Don't look up on your follow through; just make sure you get the ball out of there.

I had Byron over for dinner shortly after his first wife, Louise, passed away [in 1985]. I'd been taught his grip and his stance and his swing by Harvey [Penick] so it was fascinating to hear him talk. And he had a terrific lot to say: "You move your legs this way and this much, and you grip it like this."

Byron developed the modern technique of using the hip more and the legs more. The wood shaft swing was all hands; Byron was a swing and a hit, which was new. Now, it's everybody! All good players are in Byron's position from waist high to waist high. You move through the shot with the legs flexed through the hitting area.

1944

Frankfort-Lonsdale. 289
won $675.00 Bonds
was 5th

Essex Fells
won $503.00
was 1st.

Wyggatyl - Red cross
shot 275
won 1st
won $2675. Bonds

Chicago V tournament
shot 276
was 3rd
won $1350. Bonds
" 422. Cash

- 131 -

How do you win a lot of tournaments in a row? You just go, you just do...It just seems to click for a while. I won four in a row once and Mickey [Wright] has done it twice. But I don't know if even Byron Nelson could win eleven in a row again today, with all the pressure there'd be.

It's fun having Byron for a neighbor. Just the other day I saw him in his car at the shopping center. Peggy was going into the health-food store while I was coming out of the florist. So Byron and I chatted for a few minutes about new equipment and golf and golfers. People like him are so great, they're gonna span the decades.

—KATHY WHITWORTH

Golden Valley
won. 1st with Jug.
was 64 under Par
won $800. Bonds &
$250.00 Cash

Beverly Hills open
won 1st shot
277
Got $250. and split with
me Spahn $928.13

P.G.A.
Was finalist &
medalist with 138
Lost on 36-1 down
won $1500.00

Tam O'Shanter
68-70-73-69- 280
won 1st and $70,100.

Nashville open
64-67- 68-70- 269
1st. won $1912.50

Dallas open
69-69-70-68- 276
won by 10 strokes
won $2000.00

Portland- Oregon
74-75-73-74- 296
tied 4 th. Won $1,025.00
Bonds

San Francisco
72-71-69-69-281
won 1st and $2667.00
(includes)

Oakland
66-72-72-73-283
tied 6th won $285.00

Richmond
73-69-68-70-280
tied 3rd won 500.00

Riviera

22 tournaments
1944

1945

I don't know why, but in 1945 we were just so tuned in. It didn't matter where we were playing, we were tearing it apart. We were on a little different level than the rest of them. During one stretch I was 69 under par and Byron was 65 under. The highest I scored was 74 and the lowest was 62. And those bumpy, dormant bermuda greens weren't at all like the greens today.

1945

Riviera - L. A. 1 - 8
71 - 70 - 72 - 71 - 284
Tied 2 nd. won $600 Bucks

Phoenix 9 - 14
68 - 65 - 72 - 69. 274
1 st. won $1,333, 33 Bucks

Tucson
67 - 68 - 67 - 67 - 269
was 2 nd won $700. cash

Texas Open
67 - 66 - 68 - 68. 269
won 2 nd won $700.00 cash

Corpus Christi
66 - 63. 65 - 70. 264
won by 4 strokes. $1,000.00

We'd go to play an exhibition between tournaments and we'd have lunch with the golf committee.

"What will you shoot, Byron?" they'd ask.

Byron would say "May I see a scorecard?," and "Are these yardages honest?" Then he'd say "I believe I'll shoot a sixty-three, or a sixty-five." And then he'd do it.

I remember the tournament in Philadelphia (then McSpaden's hometown) in 1945 very well. I had very bad hay fever and asthma and was sneezing my head off the first nine holes, but I recovered and shot seven 33s in a row (73-66-66-66). However, Byron birdied the last five holes in a row for a 63 to beat me by two.

I finished second twelve or thirteen times that year. Byron figured that if I could do that today I'd win more than two million dollars. Finishing second—usually to Byron—and getting paid in war bonds didn't discourage me. I just enjoyed playing well. And Byron was my best friend.

1945

New Orleans
70 - 70 - 73 - 71 - 284 Tied
65 - 70 · Playoff metropolis
Gate   153.30

Gulfport
69 - 68 - 72 - 66 - 275
Tied Snead shot 71 in
Playoff lost on 19th hole

Pensacola
69 - 69 - 71 - 65 - 274
Second · won   700.⁰⁰

Jacksonville · Fla.
68 - 66 - 72 - 69 - 275
tied both won 285.⁰⁰

*We'd play one or two practice rounds togeth-
er, then one or two tournament rounds together,
since they put the leaders in the same group at
the end of the tournament. He traveled with
Louise, but when she went home, he traveled
with me. We never quarreled from 1933 to
1947.*

—JUG MCSPADEN

IN THE ZONE

I had people tell me that it was boring to watch
me play when I got things going in 1945. It
wasn't said in an unkindly way. It was because I
was so consistent in putting the ball on the fairway, on the green, and into the cup.

Percentage-wise, I *was* on the fairway and on
the green in regulation most of the time. On the
other hand, people get tired of that. They want to
see you hit it in the woods, a bunker, or water, and
then knock it out and make bunches of birdies

from those places. That's why Arnold Palmer was so great with the fans. Arnold made a lot of bad shots and ended up with a lot of bogeys, but he also charged it in here and there. He would fall behind in a tournament, then shoot a 65. That's why he had his army with him.

But my way of playing was fairways and greens, fairways and greens. Keep it straight, keep it safe, and capitalize on as many birdie putts as possible.

THE STREAK

On the following few pages are summaries of Byron's record eleven consecutive victories.

MIAMI INTERNATIONAL FOUR-BALL

Miami Springs C.C., Miami, Florida

March 8-11

*NOTE: Byron teamed with Jug McSpaden to win easily, ultimately
beating Sam Byrd and Denny Shute in the finals, 8 and 6.*

CHARLOTTE OPEN

Myers Park C.C., Charlotte, North Carolina

March 16-21

*NOTE: Nelson needed 36 holes in a playoff to beat Sam Snead by
four shots.*

GREATER GREENSBORO OPEN

Starmount Forest C.C., Greensboro, North Carolina

March 23-25

NOTE: Nelson won by eight strokes over Sam Byrd.

DURHAM OPEN

Hope Valley C.C., Durham, North Carolina

March 30-April 1

*NOTE: Nelson's closing 65 gave him a comeback, five-shot victory over
Toney Penna.*

Miami Four Ball

Beat Klein - Christman - 6 - 5
" Hogan - Dudley - 4 - 3
" Picard - Kroll - 3 - 2
" Byrd - Shute - 8 - 6
Won - $1100.⁰⁸

Charlotte Open
70 - 68 - 66 - 68 - 272 tied
69 tied again 6,9 won
won 13,12,50 Ruch

Greensboro, N C
70 - 67 - 68 - 66 - 271
won by 8 strokes - $1000.⁰⁰

Durham Open
71 - 69 - 71 - 65 - 276
1st by 5 strokes - won 1000.⁰⁰

$\mathcal{A}$TLANTA IRON LUNG TOURNAMENT

Capital City C.C., Atlanta, Georgia

April 5-8

NOTE: Nelson's fifth consecutive victory broke the previous record of four in a row owned by Johnny Farrell.

$\mathcal{M}$ONTREAL OPEN

Islemere Golf and C.C., Montreal, Canada

June 7-10

NOTE: Nelson recorded only one bogey over 72 holes after a two-month break in the PGA Tour schedule.

$\mathcal{P}$HILADELPHIA INQUIRER INVITATION

Llarnech C.C., Philadelphia, Pennsylvania

June 14-17

NOTE: Nelson birdied five of the last six holes for a closing 63 to edge Jug McSpaden by two.

$\mathcal{C}$HICAGO VICTORY NATIONAL OPEN

Calumet C.C., Chicago, Illinois

June 29-July 1

NOTE: Despite a sore back, Nelson survived a 36-hole Sunday finale to win by seven over Jug McSpaden and Ky Laffoon.

1945

Atlanta - Ga.
64 - 69 - 65 - 65 - 263
won by 2 strokes . won $1500.00

Montreal - Canada
63 - 68 - 69 - 68 - 268
won by 10 strokes $2000.00
Canadian
ani 1531.

Phila Open

68 - 68 - 70 - 63 269
won by 2 strokes $2500.00

Chicago V.
69 - 68 - 68 - 70 - 275
won by 7 strokes
1500.00

*P*GA Championship
Moraine C.C., Dayton, Ohio
July 9-15
NOTE: Nelson began with a 3 and 3 victory over Gene Sarazen, and later beat Sam Byrd, 3 and 2, in the finals.

*T*AM O'SHANTER ALL-AMERICAN OPEN
Tam O'Shanter C.C., Chicago, Illinois
July 26-29
NOTE: Nelson shot four rounds of 68 or better to beat runner-up Ben Hogan by eleven shots.

*C*ANADIAN OPEN
Thornhill C.C., Toronto, Canada
August 2-4
NOTE: Nelson began the last round with a large lead and won by four over Herman Barron despite shooting a final-round 72.

1945

P.G.A.   70-65
Tied medalist - 138.
   Won 125.⁰⁰
1st Beat Sargon 3-2
2nd Beat Turnesa 1 & >6
3rd Beat Shute 3-2
4th Beat Ammon 5-4
5th Beat Byrd 4-3
Won - 3500.⁰⁰

Tam O'Shanter
66- 68- 68· 67-269
won by 11 strokes 10,200.

Canadian Open
68- 72-72- 68-280
won by 4 strokes
Consolation & Won 2000.⁰⁰

THE STREAK ENDS

I had won eleven straight tournaments in 1945 and found myself playing in Memphis. That's where I really lost my concentration. I think it was because of fatigue; not physical fatigue as much as mental fatigue and so forth.

I was way behind in the last round, trailing Freddie Haas. I was charging real well on him when I got to a par-three hole on the early part of the back nine. It was about a hundred fifty yards—a full seven-iron shot. Well, I hit my ball dead on the flagstick. My ball hit it. Now in those days, they had those big wide flagsticks compared to the thin Fiberglas ones they have today. My ball bounced well away from the hole and I ended up making double bogey.

I wasn't upset about that bad break then, although I wound up losing by two strokes. I remembered thinking that I had hit a good enough shot to maybe make a two and catch Freddie. I did lose, but I was still in my zone

19 45

Spring Lake N.J.
6 9 - 71 - 140
Won by 1 stroke
$1 500.00
Pro Amateur = 684.74

Memphis Open
69 - 73 - 66 - 68 - 276
tied for 2 nd
$1,200

Knoxville Open
won pro-am - 66
67 - 69 - 73 - 67 - 276
won by 10 strokes
$2,000

Nashville Open
70 - 64 - 67 - 68 - 269
tied 2nd won $2 00.00

- 149 -

because I went to Knoxville the following week and won by ten.

Many people might not know this, but my best year, 1945, didn't end when Haas ended my winning streak at eleven. Several weeks after winning at Knoxville, I again lost my concentration at Tacoma, Washington, finishing ninth. That was my only finish out of the top five in 1945, although I bounced back pretty well. The following week in Seattle, I shot rounds of 62, 68, 63, and 66 for a four-round total of 259, which set a new seventy-two-hole record at the time.

Of all my 1945 records, perhaps one of my favorites was my fourth-round average. They didn't keep many tour-wide statistics in those days—certainly not fourth-round average, like they do today—and my fourth-round average was 67.45 for the whole year.

19 __

Dallas Open
72-   -68- 281
3rd. won $1000.⁰⁰

Tulsa Int.
73- 69- 75- 71- 288
Was 4th won $600.⁰⁰

Spokane, Wash.
66- 66- 70- 64- 266
won by 7 stks - 1503.⁰⁰

Portland open
71- 71- 67- 66- 275
2nd won $1400.⁰⁰

Tacoma
70- 69- 73- 71- 283
Tied 10th won

1945

Seattle. open
62 - 68 - 63 - 66 - 259
New Worlds record
won $1200.00

Ft. Worth open
72 - 65 - 66 - 70 - 273
won by 8 strokes. $1500.00

31 tournaments
won · 19 - Average score 68.33
won $52,511.32

- 152 -

1946

Byron Nelson...what do you say about a guy who's so special?

   But Jimmy Demaret—not Nelson or Hogan—was the big name in our house when I was growing up. My father was the golf pro at Beaumont Country Club, and he and Jimmy had double dated. Dad married Mom, and Jimmy married Adella. I was just twelve

when Byron won eleven in a row in 1945 and I didn't know how good that was.

Then, in 1946 I think it was, along came Nelson, Hogan, [Lloyd] Mangrum, and Jack Burke, Sr. to our course to play an exhibition. I didn't realize what I was seeing, I just thought they were four of Daddy's friends. Byron shot the low score that day, but I only really remember one shot: On the sixth hole, a short par four through a chute of trees, Byron hit a driver **one foot** *from the hole.*

And I didn't really see Byron until years later, when I'd turned pro, long after he'd retired from regular competition. We were paired together at Colonial and I was a little nervous...He hit the flag twice that day with full iron shots. The way he gripped the club, the way he lined up, you knew he could start the motor running again if he wanted to. He looked like a master craftsman.

—DAVE MARR

Entry	Tournaments 1946	Caddy Fee
12.50	L. A.	175.00
10.00	Frisco	200.00
10.00	San Antonio	65.00
10.00	New Orleans	88.00
10.00	Pensacola	55.00
10.00	St. Pete	61.00
	Miami	75.00
	Augusta	147.00
10.00	Houston	125.00
10.00	Ft. Worth	100.00
10.00	St. Louis	65.00
	Boston	100.00
10.00	New York	127.00
10.00	Cleveland	200.00
	Toledo	100.00
10.00	Columbus	150.00
10.00	K. C.	95.00
10.00	Victory	100.00

(over)

- 155 -

Caddy Fee   Entry

88 $\frac{00}{}$ Chicago $2.00

150 $\frac{00}{}$ Portland   5.00

$75 $\frac{00}{}$ Ft Worth   10.00

1946

L. A. Open
71-69-72-72- 284
Won by 5 Strokes
Won $200.00

Sn Francisco
73-70-72-68- 283
won by 9 strokes
won $2,250.00

~~Richmond~~
San Antonio
64-68-72-69- 273
Was 3rd - won 750.00

New Orleans
73-69-69-66- 277
won by 5 strokes -$1500.00

JUDGING DISTANCES

You've heard me discuss my love for figures.
Another knack of mine was being able to judge
distance by eye. We didn't have yardage books in
those days and trusted only in ourselves—not
our caddies—for club selection. I had studied
some about distance and perspective in judging
distances, and I believe that served me well over
the years.

One of the rules about estimating distance
for your next shot is that it's always farther across
water than it looks. I figure your eye actually sees
only about half of the water surface in front of
you. Or when you're shooting at a green fronted
by a bunker, the tendency is to figure the distance
to the back lip of the bunker, forgetting to add in
the distance of the width of the bunker and the
distance from the back of the bunker to the front
edge of the green.

What makes a green particularly hard to
judge in terms of yardage is that sometimes there

Pensacola
75 - 69 - 70 - 72 - 286
won $132.50

St. Petersburg
68 · 69 · 69 - 71 - 277
tied 5 4th 6th · won $650.00

Miami Four Ball
Beat - Klein - Goggin - 2 - 1
..   - Little - Ferguson - 4 - 3
Lost to Snead - Byrd - 41st Hole
won $300.00

Masters $356.25

is nothing in back of the green to use for perspective. I remember a number of years ago at the Masters when Tom Watson twice put his ball into the front bunker at Augusta's seventeenth. There is about fifteen feet of bunker that you can't see from back in the fairway. Same thing with the seventeenth hole at Firestone in Akron, Ohio. You're playing uphill with a little mounded bunker in the front of the green. If you don't know that and remember it, you will be that much short of the green every time.

During the war years, I knew an army colonel who was the commander of an artillery post. He played a lot of golf and I would sometimes play with him when I had the time. Every once in a while, he would ask me how far it was to the hole. I guess I impressed him with my answers because he said he had never seen anybody in the world who could judge distance as well as I could, and the secret to being a good artilleryman is being able to judge distance. But he couldn't get me to enlist in the service. I had

Houston
70 - 69 - 68 - 68 - 274
Won by 2 strokes - 2000.⁰⁰

Ft. Worth (Pro)
72 - 72 - 71 - 70 - 285
tied 9th won 520.⁰⁰

St. Louis - Western
290                    $16.67

Goodall Round Robin
+ 2 2
Was 3rd - won H30⁰⁰
15⁰⁰·⁰⁰ fr Boston
match + won 7 - 6

failed my physical and was classified 4-F. I was what is called a free bleeder.

I've heard people say about me, "He might miss a shot every now and then, but he won't ever misclub." That is one of the kindest compliments I've ever received.

Natl Open

71 - 71 - 69 - 73 - 284

Tied Ghezzi - Morgan

Tied at 72 first playoff

Morgan 72 - Ghezzi - Nelson

73 —

Won $1 2 0 7.³³

G-------- Int.

Was Second with Sam Snead

+ 14 Won 850.⁰⁰

Columbus Open

72 - 68 - 69 - 67 - 276

1st by 2 strokes Won 2500⁰⁰

K. C. Open

69 - 67 - 68 - 72 - 276

Tied 2nd Pro   Won 1433.³⁴

Yes, some people think he retired too early [at the end of 1946], but after the 1945 he had, Byron was the epitome of "What else is there for me to do?"

In 1952 and again in '56, after I got out of the service, Byron and I played exhibitions up and down the West Coast. On every first tee, Byron would say "What's the course record? Who owns it?"

One day in the car on the way to Fresno, I finally asked him why he always did that. He said "Ken, you always ask because if the home pro owns the course record, you don't break it. That pro lives there; we're just visitors." That tells you what Byron Nelson is made of.

Eddie Lowery and George Coleman (another wealthy golf patron) arranged a four-ball match in 1956 that matched Harvie Ward and me against Hogan and Nelson at Cypress Point. Boy, did we ever make some birdies that day [the pros beat the amateurs one-up on the final hole; the four combined to shoot twenty-six

Victory Open
73-69-69-68—279
Won. 2 strokes $1500.00

Lou O'Shanter
74-72-70-71-287
tied 7th. Won $1233.34

P.G.A. Portland
70- X qualifying
Beat Frank Walsh- 8-7
" Ivy Somberger - 3.2
Lost to Oliver - 1 down
Won 500.00

Ft. Worth Open
277- tied 7th
550.00

under par—some say it was the greatest four-ball match in history]. I remembered something Byron had taught me: No matter what, never let your opponent know your feelings, that his shot overwhelmed you or your own shot elated you. Something else I saw that day: as a competitor, Byron Nelson was able to be mean and tough and intimidating—and pleasant.

I was at a low ebb physically and mentally in 1961 after a car accident. But I re-read Byron's book Winning Golf and it really helped me [Venturi won the U.S. Open in 1964].

If I'm an authority on golf, it's because I was taught by Byron Nelson and played with Ben Hogan...Byron is the finest gentleman I've ever known. I just love the man.

—KEN VENTURI

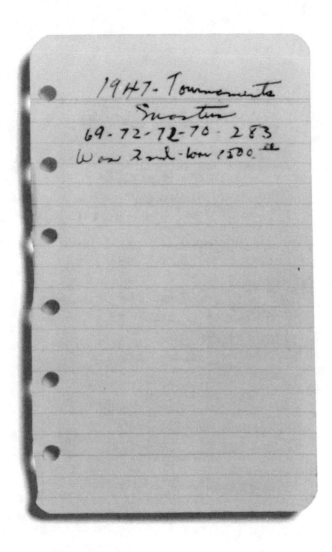

1947 - Tournaments
Snooten
69 - 72 - 72 - 70 - 283
Won 2nd - Won 1500 ⁰⁰

Appendix

Highlights
of Byron Nelson's incredible year of 1945

Total Starts:

30 (plus one unofficial event)

Total Victories:

18 (another did not count)

Consecutive Victories:

11 from March 11 through August 4; Miami Fourball, Charlotte, Greensboro, Durham, Atlanta, Montreal, Philadelphia, Chicago Victory, PGA Championship, Tam O'Shanter, Canadian.

Widest Margin of Victory:

13 strokes at Seattle (259).

Other Margins, Excluding Playoffs:

11 at Tam O'Shanter, 10 at Knoxville and Montreal, 9 at Atlanta, 8 at Greensboro and Glen Garden, 7 at Chicago Victory and Spokane, 5 at Durham, 4 at Corpus Christi and Canadian, 2 at Phoenix and Philadelphia.

Low Score:
259 at Seattle (Won with 62-68-63-66 and was 21 under par)

High Winning Score:
284 at New Orleans (70-70-73-71, four under par, winning in playoff).

Average 72-Hole Score:
273.46

Average 72-Hole Score, 16 Stroke-Play Victories:
271.2

Highest Score During Year:
288 at Tulsa (73-69-75-71, four over par to finish fourth).

Most Strokes Under Par:
22 at Spokane (Won with 66-66-70-64—266).

Subpar 72-Hole Scores:
24 of the 28 at stroke play - 86 percent (excludes Miami Fourball at better-ball partnership and PGA Championship at match play)

Even-Par, 72-Hole Scores:
2: Los Angeles (284 to finish second), Canadian Open (won with 280).

Over-Par, 72-Hole Scores:
> 2: Tulsa (288, four over par, to finish fourth),
> Tacoma (283, three over par to finish ninth).

Highest 72-Hole Finish:
> Ninth at Tacoma.

Playoffs:
> 3—at New Orleans (defeated Harold McSpaden
> 65-70), Gulfport (lost to Sam Snead 71-4 to 71-
> 5), Charlotte (defeated Snead 69-69 to 69-73).

Total Stroke-Play Rounds:
> 112 (excluding Miami Fourball, PGA
> Championship and playoffs).

Subpar Rounds:
> 88 (79 percent).

Even-Par Rounds:
> 9 (one 69, three 70s, three 71s, two 72s).

Par-or-Better Rounds:
> 97 (87 percent).

Over-Par Rounds:
> 15 (13 percent—four 71s, five 72s, five 73s, one
> 75).

Rounds in 60s:
> 74 (66 percent), excluding three more in playoffs.

Rounds in 60s, Consecutive:
  12 beginning with fourth round at Phoenix: 69,
  67, 68, 67, 67, 67, 66, 68, 68, 66, 63, 65 (44
  under par). Another streak of 11 in a row beginning with fourth round at Durham: 65, 64, 69,
  65, 65, 63, 68, 69, 68, 68, 68 (42 under par).

Rounds in 70s:
  38 (34 percent).

Rounds in 70s, Consecutive:
  4 at Los Angeles (71-72-70-71) and New
  Orleans (70-70-73-71).

Par-or-Better Rounds, Consecutive:
  22 beginning with fourth round at Durham and
  extending through first round at Canadian Open.
  He was 83 under par in that run.

Over-Par Rounds, Consecutive:
  2 in Canadian Open (72-72) and Tacoma (73-
  71).

Low Round:
  62 at Seattle in first round (8 under par).

High Round:
  75 at Tulsa in third round (4 over par).

Low Start:
  62 at Seattle.

High Start:
>73 at Tulsa (2 over par).

Low Fourth-Round Finish:
>63 at Philadelphia, seven under par (he won by two with 269).

High Fourth-Round Finish:
>71 at Los Angeles (even par), New Orleans (one under par), Tulsa (even par), Tacoma (one over par).

Fourth-Round Finishes in 60s:
>21 of the 28 events at stroke play (75 percent).

Fourth-Round Finishes in 70s:
>7 (three 70s, four 71s—25 percent).

Average Finishing Round:
>67.68 (excluding Miami Fourball and PGA Championship).

Average Finishing Round During 11-Victory Streak:
>66.67 (excluding Miami Fourball and PGA).

Average Finishing Round in Seven Remaining Victories:
>68.1.

Average Finishing Round in 16 Stroke-Play Victories:

67.3.

Best Comeback:

He was five back at New Orleans with 18 holes remaining and made it up with a closing 71, winning in a playoff.

Most Money Won, One Event :

$13,600 in war bonds at Tam O'Shanter (cash equivalent: $10,200).

Least Money Won, One Event:

$325 in war bonds at Tacoma (cash equivalent: $245).

Breakdown of the 112 Rounds Nelson Played, Excluding Playoffs:

62 - 1	66 - 13	69 - 13	72 - 8
63 - 4	67 - 10	70 - 13	73 - 5
64 - 3	68 - 23	71 - 11	75 - 1
65 - 7			

Nelson's "Ringer Rounds" for 1945:

Low: 62-63-63-63—251
High: 73-73-75-71—292

Byron Nelson's Three Fabulous Years (1944-46)

| Year | FINISHES | | | | | | SCORING | | | |
	Starts	1st	2nd	3rd	4th 5th	6th 9th	Rds	Ave.	72-hole Low	72-hole High
1944	23	9	6	5	1	2	84	69.71	269	296
1945	31	*19	7	1	2	2	112	68.37	259	288
1946	21	6	3	4	2	5	64	70.13	273	290
TOTALS	75	34	16	10	5	9	260	69.23	267	291.3

*includes unofficial victory

Nelson in the 75 Starts in the Three Years:
Won 34 times
    (45 percent of the time)
Finished first or second 50 times
    (67 percent—2 of every 3 starts)
Finished among top three 60 times
    (80 percent of the time)
Finished among top five 65 times
    (87 percent of the time)
Finished among top nine 74 times
    (99 percent of the time)

Nelson's Worst Finishes:
1944   6th, Philadelphia; tied for 6th, Oakland
1945   Tied for 9th, Tacoma
1946   Tied for 13th, Pensacola

Nelson's Most Decisive Victories:
1944   Texas, 10 strokes (with 276)
1945   Seattle, 13 strokes (with 259)
1946   San Francisco, 9 strokes (with 283)

(Statistical analysis provided by Bill Inglish)